Studies in
1 Thessalonians

I0164859

Michael Penny

ISBN: 978-1-78364-500-8

www.obt.org.uk

THE OPEN BIBLE TRUST
Fordland Mount, Upper Basildon,
Reading, RG8 8LU, UK.

Studies in 1 Thessalonians

Contents

Preface

Preface

1 Thessalonians was the subject of the mid-week evening Bible study at Grace Church, New Berlin, Wisconsin. The discussions were lively and wide-ranging and differing suggestions were put forward by friends as to the interpretation of certain passages. I am indebted to the group for their input and these *Studies in 1 Thessalonians* were written after we had finished studying the letter. However, what is contained here reflects my own current understanding and not necessarily that of the group. My hope in publishing these studies is that they may be of interest and help to a wider audience. My prayer is that all who read them will have a greater understanding of God's purposes and a deeper appreciation of His grace, so freely available to all who put their trust in our Lord and Saviour, Jesus Christ.

Michael Penny

Background
to
1 Thessalonians

Background

Familiarity with the background to 1 Thessalonians will help the reader gain a better understanding of Paul's writings to the believers there. To gain this we need only consider certain parts of the Acts of the Apostles.

Paul's second journey – Acts 15:36-16:10

At the end of Acts 15 we read that Silas was to accompany Paul on his second journey, the purpose of which was to see how those Paul had previously visited were doing. They travelled through Syria and Cilicia strengthening the churches, before coming to Derbe and Lystra, where Timothy lived. He joined the others and the group went throughout the region of Phrygia and Galatia.

In some way or other the Holy Spirit prevented them from preaching the word in the province of Asia so when they came to the border of Mysia they tried to enter Bithynia. Again the Spirit prevented them so they passed by Mysia and went down to the coastal town of Troas.

There Paul had a vision of a man of Macedonia standing and begging him to "Come over to Macedonia and help us". They concluded that God had called them to preach the Gospel there so they got ready at once to leave.

Philippi – Acts 16:11-40

From Troas they said for the island of Samothrace and then on to the Macedonian port of Neapolis. A few miles inland was

Philippi, a Roman colony and the leading city of the district of Macedonia. They were there for several days.

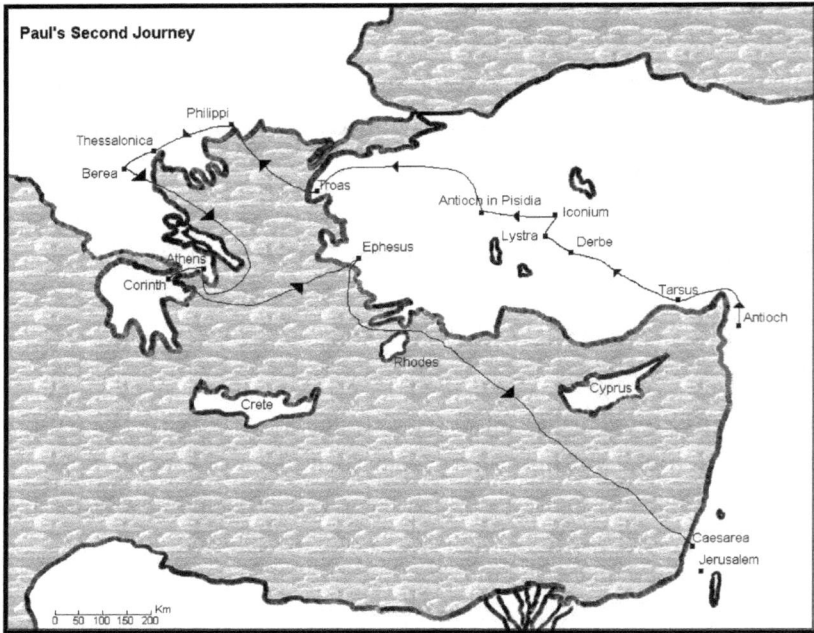

Paul's Second Journey

On the Sabbath they went outside the city gate and visited the river where they expected to find a place of prayer. Evidently there were insufficient Jews in this Roman colony for the community to have a synagogue. In such places, they gathered outside of the city on the Sabbath.

There they met a number of people including Lydia, a dealer in purple from the city of Thyatira. She believed, becoming the first recorded European convert of Paul and his party.

However, Paul and Silas soon ran into trouble. By freeing a fortune-telling slave girl from the spirit which possessed her, they incurred the wrath of her masters. They were dragging before the magistrates, stripped, beaten and imprisoned.

A midnight earthquake loosed their chains and led to the conversion of the jailer. The next day they were freed and returned to Lydia's house before continuing their journey.

Thessalonica – Acts 17:1-9

From Philippi they passed through Amphipolis and Apollonia before coming to Thessalonica, where there was a Jewish synagogue. As was his custom Paul went there and on three Sabbath days reasoned with the people from the Scriptures, explaining and proving that the Christ had to suffer and rise from the dead. "This Jesus I am proclaiming to you is the Christ," said Paul. Some of the Jews were persuaded and joined Paul and Silas, as did a large number of God-fearing Greeks and not a few prominent women.

However, the Jews who had not been persuaded that Jesus was the Christ (Messiah) were jealous. They rounded up some bad characters from the market-place, formed a mob and started a riot in the city. They failed to find Paul and Silas but found Jason, in whose house they had been staying. The hostile Jews dragged Jason and some other brothers before the city officials, accusing them, amongst other things, of "defying Caesar's decrees, saying that there is another king, one called Jesus". When they heard this the crowd and the city officials were thrown into a turmoil. However, bail was put up for Jason and his fellow-Christians and they were let go.

But it would seem that the hostile non-Christian Jews wanted Paul, and possibly Silas. As soon as it was night the brothers sent these two away.

Berea – Acts 17:10-15

Paul and Silas were sent to Berea. On arriving they went straight to the Jewish synagogue and had a totally different reception. There the Jews were more noble than those at Thessalonica, possibly being better educated and more comfortably off. They received the message with great eagerness and examined the scriptures *every day*, not just on the Sabbaths, wanting to see if what Paul had said about the Christ having to suffer was true. As a result many of the Jews believed, as did also a number of the prominent Greek women and many Greek men.

However, this happy time was to be short lived for when the non-Christian Jews in Thessalonica learned that Paul was preaching the word of God at Berea, they went there, agitating the crowds and stirring them up. The brothers immediately sent Paul to the coast, but Silas and Timothy stayed at Berea.

Athens – Acts 17:15-34

The men who accompanied Paul through Berea brought him to Athens and then left with instructions for Silas and Timothy to join him as soon as possible. It would seem from 1 Thessalonians 3:1-2 that Timothy did join Paul in Athens for a short while, before Paul sent him back to Thessalonica to strengthen and encourage them.

Corinth – Acts 18:1-17

From Athens Paul journeyed the few miles to Corinth where he reasoned in the synagogue every Sabbath, trying to persuade the Jews and the Greeks that Jesus was the Christ. When there, Silas and Timothy came from Macedonia (Acts 18:5) and it would seem that it was at this point that Paul first wrote to the Thessalonians. He mentions them both in the opening verse of the letter and states in 1 Thessalonians 3:6 that "Timothy has *just now* come to us from you and brought good news about your faith and your love."

It would appear that he also brought news of the problems and difficulties, the doubts and fears, the uncertainties and misgivings, of the Thessalonian believers. We can imagine how these people had suffered from what we have learned. Certainly the non-Christian Jews at Thessalonica seem to have been one of the most hostile groups of which we read. Their actions against Christians took them outside their own city. They were prepared to travel to Berea, and maybe even further, in their pursuit of those who taught that Jesus was the Christ.

In this first letter to the Thessalonians Paul deals with some of their worries. He gives advice to alleviate their problems and difficulties, provides encouragement to remove their doubts and fears, and includes some sound teaching to overcome their uncertainties and misgivings. As such there is much in the five chapters to help Christians in all ages.

2 Thessalonians

It would seem that the first letter to the Thessalonians was written and dispatched soon after Timothy and Silas joined Paul in Corinth. Paul resided there for eighteen months and further news from Thessalonica resulted in him having to write a second letter. Again Timothy and Silas are mentioned in the introduction and it is generally thought that his second letter to these hard-pressed Christians was also written from Corinth, but probably nearer to the end of his stay.

Paul's third journey

We can see Paul's care and concern for these people not only from his letters, but also from his desire to visit them again. On his third journey Paul was in Ephesus for two years, but decided to return to Jerusalem via Macedonia, which is in the opposite direction! He sent Timothy and Erastus on ahead of him (Acts 19:10, 21-22) before travelling north to Macedonia and then south to Greece. Then, when he was about to sail from Greece to Jerusalem, he discovered that the non-Christian Jews had made a plot against him and so returned to Macedonia (Acts 20:1-5).

Summary

Paul's initial period with these people may have been short, being little more than three weeks, due to the hostility of the Jews who did not accept Jesus was the Messiah. He had great concern for the Thessalonian believers in their difficult situation. At his direction Timothy and Silas stayed in the area when he had to leave Berea. Timothy reported on their welfare to him at Athens and then returned. When further problems and difficulties arose Timothy and Silas went to Corinth and related them to Paul, who immediately wrote his first letter to them. Some months later there was more distressing news so a second letter was dispatched. Then, on his third journey, Paul visited them twice more. Leaving Ephesus he travelled north to Macedonia and then south to Greece. From there he went back through Macedonia and sailed from Philippi.

1 Thessalonians

Chapter 1

Chapter 1

Paul, Silas and Timothy. To the church of the Thessalonians in God the Father and the Lord Jesus Christ: Grace and peace to you. (1:1)

In our background introduction we saw that Silas and Timothy joined Paul when he was in Corinth (Acts 18:5) and that this letter was written shortly afterwards.

In Thessalonica Paul proclaimed that Jesus is the Christ and again, in our background introduction, we saw that "Some of the Jews were persuaded and joined Paul and Silas, as did a large number of the God-fearing Greeks and not a few prominent women." These God-fearing Greeks were not pagan Gentiles, but ones who had taken it upon themselves to sit in the synagogues to hear the Scriptures being read. For some this was a first step to becoming a Proselyte: i.e. one of another nation who became a Jew by being circumcised, observing the Sabbath, and keeping the Mosaic Law.

Paul's greeting to the church at Thessalonica, with its Jews and God-fearing Greeks, was "Grace and peace". The Hebrew for peace is *shalom* and, as many know, is the standard Hebrew greeting. Here, in Greek, it is *eirene*. The standard Greek greeting was *charis*, "grace". Thus with "grace and peace" Paul makes one greeting out of the two used by the different sections of the church.

We always thank God for all of you, mentioning you in our prayers. We continually remember before our God and Father your work produced

by faith, your labour prompted by love, and your
endurance inspired by hope in our Lord Jesus
Christ. (1:2-3)

When we think of what these Thessalonian believers underwent, the fear they must have had when they saw the hostility of the non-Christian Jews towards Paul and Silas, then we can appreciate Paul's prayers for them. He remembered, particularly, their, "work produced by faith", their "labour prompted by love", and their "endurance inspired by hope in our Lord Jesus Christ". What lessons there are in these words for believers today. To be fruitful in works, labour and endurance, we need a solid grounding in faith, hope and love.

Exhorting new believers to work, to labour and to endure may be fruitless. These are the fruits that grow out of faith, out of love and out of hope. If any brother or sister is failing to display the good works, or is no longer laboring, or has little endurance, then he or she needs to be taught more about faith, hope and love, rather than to be exhorted to works, labour and endurance. If they have the former, the latter should follow.

Brothers loved by God, we know that he has
chosen you, because out gospel came to you not
simply with words, but also with power, with the
Holy Spirit and with deep conviction. You know
how we lived among you for your sake. You
became imitators of us and of the Lord; in spite
of severe suffering, you welcomed the message
with the joy given by the Holy Spirit. And so
became a model to all the believers in
Macedonia and Achaia. (1:4-7)

In Acts we have no record of Paul working any miracles in Thessalonica. However, he says that the gospel came not simply with words, but also with power (*dunamis*), a word sometimes linked with the miraculous and the Holy Spirit. It is possible that, as with other places mentioned in Acts, some form of miraculous outpouring from the Holy Spirit did take place. It was common at that time.

It would appear that the Holy Spirit also gave them joy, and they needed if for they suffered much; the non-Christian Jews in Thessalonica being some of the most hostile Paul met on his travels. Yet in spite of their sufferings they became imitators of Christ and a model to all believers in their area. Would it not be wonderful if the same could be said of us?

> *The Lord's message rang out from you not only in Macedonia and Achaia – your faith in God has become known everywhere. Therefore we do not need to say anything about it, for they themselves report what kind of reception you gave us. They tell how you turned to God from idols to serve the living and true God, and to wait for his Son form heaven, whom he raised from the dead – Jesus, who rescues us from the coming wrath. (1:8-10)*

These Thessalonians were a model to all the believers in Macedonia and Achaia. Not only was this with respect to their works, labour, and endurance, it was also that the Lord's message rang out from them, but not only in Macedonia and Achaia. It was everywhere. Their faith in God had become known to all.

So, too, had the reception they had given Paul, Timothy and Silas, and the fact that they had turned form idols. It would seem, here, that Paul has in mind the God-fearing Greeks who became believers, rather than the Jews who had accepted Christ. The former had a background in idolatry. The latter did not. However, although there is no record in Acts of Paul addressing any pagan Gentiles in Thessalonica, it is possible that some of the converts to Christ had come straight out of idolatry into Christianity, without becoming God-fearers who sat at the back of the synagogues. If this is the case, then we can understand the reason for Paul's lavish praise.

These had turned from idols to serve the living and true God and to wait for his Son from heaven. It is this return of Christ which may be behind Paul's words in 1:3, when he writes of their endurance being inspired by hope in the Lord Jesus Christ. Their hope was the return of Christ and His rescuing them from the wrath of God. This wrath, the subject of Revelation and other prophetic Scriptures, is to fall upon those who oppose God and so by accepting Christ they would be saved from it. This, to them, was a grave reality. They believed and expected it to happen in their lifetime, and it could have!

We read in Acts of the Apostles that Christ was to return soon, provided the Jews repented, turned to God and accepted Jesus as the Messiah. If they had done so then the times of refreshing would have come from the Lord. He would have sent Christ and everything would have been restored (Acts 3:19-21). This is mentioned in many of the letters written during the Acts period, probably within a few years of Thessalonians. We read of it in such passages as James 5:8-9, where it states that "the Lord's coming is near." Peter writes that "the end of all things is near" (1 Peter 4:7) and John that "this is the last hour" (1 John 2:18).

Hebrews10:37 says that "in just a very little while, He who is coming will come and will not delay"; Romans 13:12 "the night is nearly over; the day is almost here' and 1 Corinthians 10:11 "the fulfillment of the ages has come".

However, the passage which most graphically illustrates the situation is 1 Corinthians 7, written a few years after Thessalonians. There Paul advises against marriage for single people (v27) and against having children for married couples (v29). The reason for this is "because of the present crisis" (v26), "because the time is short" (v29). In all this Paul says a little more than Christ does when speaking of the great distress which should precede His second coming (Matthew 24:21, 29-30). Of those living in Jerusalem and Judea, our Saviour states "How dreadful it will be in those days for pregnant women and nursing mothers!"

Thus what the Thessalonians were looking forward to, at the time Paul wrote to them, was the return of Christ within their lifetime. However, before such an event there was to be the great distress which was primarily to affect the Jews in Jerusalem and Judea (Matthew 24:15-16), but which would, no doubt, have its repercussions elsewhere. (I have dealt with this more fully in *Signs of the Second Coming* published by the Open Bible Trust.)

In the course of time this situation changed. At the end of Acts we read of Israel being blind and deaf due to hardening their hearts against the Lord Jesus. As such they lost their nationalist privileges and blessings which went with the old covenant. God's plan for his people took a different course. It was now to be centred in all nations, instead of one (Acts 28:26-28). After this change Paul wrote seven letters – Ephesians, Philippians, Colossians, 1 & 2 Timothy, Titus and Philemon. None of these says anything unambiguously about the nearness of Christ's return. They do not even mention His "coming", *parousia*. However, when we read Thessalonians we must keep in mind that at the time Paul wrote that letter, Christ's near return was a real possibility for his readers, as was the wrath of God upon those who opposed him.

1 Thessalonians

Chapter 2

Chapter 2

You know, brothers, that our visit to you was not a failure. We had previously suffered and being insulted and Philippi, as you know, but with the help of our God we dared to tell you his gospel in spite of strong opposition. (2:1-2)

The visit to Thessalonica had been a short one, they being there but three Sabbaths (Acts 17:2). That this is, however, was not a failure. On the contrary it had been a success and since then they had been nurtured by Silas and Timothy, and by the prayers of Paul and others.

The insult suffered at Philippi is recorded in Acts 16:16-40. Paul and Silas, although Roman citizens, had been beaten publicly and thrown into a prison without a trial. This was a result of freeing a slave-girl from the spirit which possessed him. Her owners to were upset at losing money and so dragged Paul and Silas into the market place to face the authorities.

The strong opposition faced at Thessalonica came from a different source; namely Jews who refused to believe that Jesus was the Messiah (Acts 17:1-9). This group was so hostile that of they pursued Paul to the Berea and spoil the work there (Acts 17:10-15). Yet in spite of such opposition Paul preached the gospel. What an example he is to us today, who are often too afraid to even mention the name of our Saviour at our place of work, to talk about Him to our friends or witness to Him amongst our neighbours.

*For the appeal we make does not spring from
error or impure motives, nor are we trying to
trick you. On the contrary, we speak of men
approved by God to be entrusted with the gospel.
We are not trying to please men by God, who test
our hearts. You know we never used flattery, nor
did we put on a mask to cover up greed   - God
our witness. We are not looking for praise from
men, not from you for anyone else. (2:3-6)*

The word "appeal" is *paraklesis* which, according to *The
Companion Bible,* comes from *parakaleo* meaning "to call aside,
appealed to (by way of exhortation, entreaty, comfort, or
instruction)". It is translated "encouragement" in Acts 4:36.

In writing to the Thessalonians Paul was doing all these, and
more. However, he felt the need to assert that he was doing so,
not there any underhand reasons. Why he should feel the need to
state this is hard to say. Perhaps in his absence his character had
been attacked by the non-Christian Jews. They may have
suggested that some of these things Paul conveyed through
Timothy were merely flattery, that he was commending them
simply to please them, that he was really after their money and
that he had taken nothing while he was there because he had been
there is such a short time and had not asked for anything merely
to cover up his real purpose. Paul sets about refuting this by first
urging them to recall that he never used flattery. Then he lives:

*As apostles of Christ we could have been a
burden to you, but we would gentle among you,
like a mother caring for her little children. We
loved you so much that we delighted to share
with you not only the gospel of God by our lives*

as well, because you had become so dear to us.
Sure you remember, brothers, our toil and
hardship; we worked night and day in order not
to be a burden to anyone what we preach the
gospel of God to you.

  You are witnesses, and so is God, of how
holy, righteous and blameless so we were among
we were among you who believed. For you know
that we dealt with each of you as her father deals
with his children, encouraging, comforting and
urging you to live lives worthy of God, it calls
you into his kingdom and glory. (2:7-12)

In Acts 18:3-5 we read of Paul in Corinth making tents with
Aquila and Priscilla. He continued to do this to earn money until
the arrival of Timothy and Silas, who probably supported the
group in this or some other way. As a result Paul and his party
were not a financial burden to the Corinthians church, but Paul
had to remind them of this (2 Corinthians 11:9; 12: 13-16).
Similarly he had to remind the Thessalonians that he had been no
burden to them either, though as apostles of Christ they could
have been, and perhaps should have been, supported (see 3 John
5-7 and 1 Timothy 5:17-18). Rather than receiving, they had been
like parents to the Thessalonians; giving, encouraging,
comforting, urging. Indeed they shared their lives with them.

It is a sad situation when opponents you cannot adequately argue
against the message turn their attention to the messenger and
attacked him. This is what the non - Christian Jews did to Paul
and he was forced to take recourse to defend himself. If this has
ever happened to us, and sadly it does happen in Christian circles,
then we can sympathize with Paul. The let us learn a lesson and
never do it to others.

And we also thank God continually because,
when you receive the word of God, which you
heard from us, you accepted it not as the word of
men, but as it actually is, the word of God, which
is at work in you who believe. (2:13)

The Thessalonians accepted Paul's words is the word of God.
This was right. He had been chosen to take God's message to the
Gentiles (Acts 9:15; Galatians 2; 7-9). He was God's apostle and
minister to the Gentiles (Romans 11: 13; 15:16) and Peter
considered his writings as part of Scripture (2 Peter 3:15-16). At
that time God conveyed send gifts upon men, making you
apostles or prophets or teachers. Indeed, they had been appointed
by the Holy Spirit (Acts 20:28) and when filled by the Holy Spirit
what they said was the word of God. Although some claim such
divine origins are their words today, the situation is otherwise. In
Paul's later letters we see him insisting that overseers and
servants must be people who are able to teach (1 Timothy 3:2; 2
Timothy 2:24). He also instructs Timothy to entrust all that Paul
has heard to "reliable man who will be qualified to teach others"
(2 Timothy 2:2). And he gives both Timothy and Titus advice on
the type of people to leadership positions (1 Timothy 3:1-13;
Titus 1:5-9). No one today he can claim, as Paul and others did
then, that they are appointed by the God and that their words are
other word of God.

For you, brothers, became imitators of God's
church is in Judea, which are in Christ Jesus:
You suffered from the Jews, who kill the Lord
Jesus in the prophets and also drove us out. They
displeased God and are hostile to all men in their
effort to keep us from speaking to the Gentiles so
that they may be saved. In this way they always

heap up their sins to the limit. The wrath of God
has come upon them as last. (2:14-16)

The greatest persecution that Judean churches had suffered up to then had come from the hands of Saul of Tarsus. After his conversion of the Christian Jews enjoyed at time of peace (Acts 9:31). We do not read it in Acts of much further opposition, but clearly it continued. Paul suffered at the hands of the Jews in Damascus and Jerusalem (Acts 9:23-30). Herod's execution of James in the arrest of other believers please the non-Christian Jews, so he ceased Peter also (Acts 12:1-3). And here, in Thessalonians, Paul mentions such suffering to comfort the believers there, letting them know they are not alone in this.

However, Paul had suffered great opposition from the Jews on his journeys and so, too, had the churches he founded. Elymas, a Jewish sorcerer opposed him in Cyprus. Many non-Christian Jews rose up at Pisidian Antioch expelled Paul and Barnabas from their region (Acts 13:6-8, 50). Some plotted to start number at Iconium. At Lystra Paul was stoned (Acts 14:5, 19). At Thessalonica Jewish opposition was great in spread over to Berea (Acts 17: 5, 13).

However, in all this the Jews were not behaving out of character. They had killed the Lord Jesus. They had killed the prophets. Now they were driving Paul out, and attempting to kill him. Nothing had changed. In such behaviour they displeased God, but it was a new hostility that was to bring about their downfall. This related to their efforts to prevent Paul from speaking to the Gentiles and taking them the message of salvation.

When we read through the Acts of the Apostles we find its earlier chapters dedicated solely to the people of Israel. There is no

Gentile convert until Cornelius in chapter 10, and no further ones until Acts 11:19-21. Then, in Acts 13:2-4, Paul and Barnabas leave on their first journey, taking them to the other nations.

In Romans 11 Paul explains the reason why he was sent to the Gentiles. It was that "salvation has come to the Gentiles *to make Israel envious*" and it was his hope "that I may somehow *arouse my own people* to envy and save some of them" (Romans 11:11, 14). He goes on to paint a picture of Israel as an old olive tree from which some branches are taken and grafted into the cultivated olive tree of Israel. In nature the vigorous wild olive would stimulate, arouse, and provoke the cultivated one into bearing fruit. By sending Paul to the Gentiles with the message of salvation, this was just what God was doing to Israel. He was arousing them, stimulating them. All in hope that they would be provoked into accepting Christ themselves (Romans 11:17-25).

In Acts we see this provocation. At Pisidian Antioch when the Jews saw the crowds who gathered to hear Paul they were filled with jealousy and talked abusively against what Paul said (Acts 13:45). Similarly in Thessalonica, those Jews who did not accept that Jesus was the Christ were jealous when they saw that not only were some Jews persuaded, but so, too, were a large number of God-fearing Greeks (Acts 17:4-5).

It was such opposition as this that heaped up their sins to the limit. The figure here has its origins in the Old Testament. There God promised Abraham a land for his descendants. However, they could not possess it until the fourth generation because "the sin of the Amorites had not yet reached its full measure" (Genesis 15:16).

It was the same with the Jewish generation of the New Testament to whom Christ said, "Fill up, then, the measure of sin of your forefathers!" (Matthew 23:32). Their greatest sin was their rejection and crucifixion of Christ. However, that sin had not filled their cup of iniquity. Their hostility to all me and their efforts to keep Paul and others form preaching salvation to the Gentiles had heaped up their sins to the limit This was how the non-Christian Jews at Thessalonica had behaved. Now they could not escape the wrath of God which is to fall upon those who oppose Him. And what was true of the Thessalonian Jews was soon to be true of the nation of Israel. At the end of Acts Paul quotes the sad prophecy of Isaiah 6 for the last time. Israel had so opposed the work among the Gentiles and had hardened its heart against Christ that it had become blind and deaf to any further message. As Such God's salvation was sent to the Gentiles (Acts 28:25-28).

> But, brothers, when we were torn away from you
> for a short time (in person, not in thought), out of
> our intense longing we made every effort to see
> you. For we wanted to come to you – certainly I,
> Paul, did, again and again – but Satan stopped us.
> For what is our hope, our joy, or the crown in
> which we will glory in the presence of our Lord
> Jesus Christ when he comes? Is it not you? Indeed.
> You are our glory and joy. (2:17-20)

Here Paul refers to his hasty departure from Thessalonica recorded in Acts 17:5-10. On morning all was well. During the day things turned sour at the hands of the non-Christian Jews. That night Paul and Silas were sent to Berea. Yet, although they may have been torn away in person, his thoughts were often with them and he had wanted to return. It would seem that he attempted to on more than one occasion, probably while he was at Athens for there would have been frequent boats from the nearby port of Pireaus. However, he had been prevented from doing so by Satan. What shape this satanic opposition took, we are not told. It may have been the continued hostility of the Thessalonian Jews. But in spite of such opposition, Paul wanted to see them and had made several efforts to do so. Such intense longing and efforts sprang from his deep affection and respect for them. He describes them as his glory and joy.

1 Thessalonians

Chapter 3

Chapter 3

So when we could stand it no longer, we thought it best to be left by ourselves in Athens. We sent Timothy, who is our brother and God's fellow worker in spreading the gospel of Christ, to strengthen and encourage you in your faith, so that no-one would be unsettled by these trials. You know quite well that we were destined for them. In fact when we were with you, we kept telling you that we would be persecuted. And it turned out that way, as you well know. For this reason, when I could stand it no longer, I sent to find out about your faith. I was afraid that in some way the tempter might have tempted you and our efforts might have been in vain. (3:1-5)

In Acts 17:14-15 we read that when opposition arose at Berea, from the hands of the non-Christian Jews of Thessalonica, the brothers sent Paul to the coast while Silas and Timothy stayed on. Those who accompanied Paul took him to Athens and he left instructions for Silas and Timothy to join him there as soon as possible. It would seem that Timothy did join Paul in Athens, but however much Paul enjoyed his company, in the end he sent him back to Thessalonica for Paul was so concerned for the believers there. Timothy's work was to strengthen and encourage them in their trials.

Paul wrote to remind them to expect trials, that they were destined for them, and that he expected to be persecuted. After Paul's conversion God told Ananias that He would show Paul "how much he must suffer in my name" (Acts 9:16) and Paul may have recounted this vision to the Thessalonians. Also, because Paul was an apostle, he may have had the gift of prophecy and so knew that opposition was to arise in Thessalonica. (cf. Agabus in Acts 21:1-11). On the other hand, it may have been just simple experience. Paul had been opposed everywhere else he had been and he saw the signs of impending hostility in Thessalonica. Whichever it may have been, Paul had warned them of the impending trials. They were now suffering from them, but Paul was in Athens. How were they coping? When he could stand it no longer, he sent Timothy to strengthen them, instructing him to return with the news.

> *But Timothy has just now come to us from you and has brought good news about your faith and love. He has told us that you always have pleasant memories of us and that you long to see us, just as we also long to see you. Therefore, brothers, in all our distress and persecution we are encouraged about you because of your faith. For now we really live, since you are standing firm in the Lord. How can we thank God enough for you in return for all the joy we have in the presence of our God because of you. (3:6-9)*

The news Timothy brought back was truly good news. Paul's fears were unfounded on two counts. First the Thessalonians were standing firm in the Lord and their faith was strong, in spite of opposition form the non-Christian Jews. Also they had pleasant memories of Paul and longed to see him. The possible character assassination, which may have been behind Paul's need to defend himself (2:3-12), had fallen on deaf ears. Thus Paul had great joy, so much so that he could hardly thank God enough for them.

Night and day we pray most earnestly that we may see you again and supply what is lacking in your faith. Now may our God and Father himself and our Lord Jesus clear the way for us to come to you. May the Lord make your love increase and overflow for each other and for everyone else, just as ours does for you. May he strengthen your hearts so that you will be blameless and holy in the presence of our God and Father when our Lord Jesus come with all his holy ones. (3:10-13)

In what way were the Thessalonian believers lacking in faith? The word "supply" in the NIV is translated "perfect" in the KJV and may be best understood in the sense of "maturing". Paul's desire was for them to grow in faith, to be spiritually mature.

This is the fourth time he has mentioned their faith in this chapter. First, in v 2, Timothy was sent to strengthen and encourage their faith. Then in v 5, Paul wanted to know the state of their faith. In v 6 Timothy brought good news about their faith yet, v 10, something was still lacking in their faith. What, precisely, it may have been we do not know. It may have be linked to issues dealt with in chapter's 4 and 5, both practical and doctrinal ones. The former related to living a life pleasing to God and exhibiting brotherly love. Were they convinced that this was what God wanted? The latter concerned such matters as whether God could raise the dead. No doubt Paul had taught them that He could and would, but they appear to have been uncertain as to whether this was the case and they were unclear as to what would be the situation when Christ returned.

I am sure many of us today need our faith enlarged and expanded, just as the Thessalonians did. Do we believe the quality of our moral lives and our love for one another are crucial to our Saviour's will for us? And what of prophecy and the events surrounding Christ's return? Have we a clear picture? We may have a clear picture, but is it an accurate one?

It seems that Paul was still unable to go to Thessalonica. This may be due to continued satanic opposition (2:18) and so he prays for the Lord to clear the way. He also asks the Lord to increase their love for one another, but not only for one another, but for everyone else. This is certainly a prayer we all need to pray.

Verse 13 may appear to contradict Ephesians 1:4 and Colossians 1:22. There we read that believers have been chosen "to be holy and blameless" in God's sight, that they are to be presented "holy in his sight, without blemish and free from accusation". However, these two verses express a future purpose rather than a present experience. We should aim at being in ourselves what we are already in God's sight and intention. This is the thrust of Paul's prayer for the Thessalonians and it is a prayer believers today can offer for one another.

Finally Paul makes another reference to the coming (*parousia*) of Christ. He has done so in 1:10 and 2:20. He does so again here, and will do so in 4:15-17 and again in chapter 5. This shows us how important a subject this was for the Thessalonian believers at that time. As said earlier, His return during their life-time was a possibility and, understandably, it greatly concerned both them and Paul.

The reference to "holy ones" is ambiguous. Some see this as referring to angels, but the word is *hagios*, generally translated "saints" and only here translated "holy ones" by the *NIV*. That Christ will be accompanied with angels when He returns is true

(Matthew 16:27; 24:30-31; 25:31). However, in this verse Paul is more likely to be reminding his readers of the coming of the Lord Jesus with all His saints. This would prepare them for what Paul is soon to write. "We believe that God will bring with Jesus those who have fallen asleep in him" (1 Thessalonians 4:14).

1 Thessalonians

Chapter 4

Chapter 4

Finally brothers, we instructed you how to live in order to please God, as in fact you are living. Now we ask you and urge you in the Lord Jesus to do more and more. You know what instructions we gave you by the authority of the Lord Jesus (4:1-2)

Here we read that Paul acknowledges as a fact that the Thessalonians are living lives pleasing to God. In view of what we are about to read, this may surprise us. However, it is clear that there was still room for much improvement and he urged them to do more and more.

He also refers to some instructions he gave them; instructions that come from one who spoke the word of God, one who was God's minister and apostle to the Gentiles. What those instructions were we may not know for certain, but it appears as if Paul repeats them in the coming verses.

It is God's will that you should be holy; that you should avoid sexual immorality; that each of you should learn to control his own body in a way that is holy and honourable, not in passionate lust like that of the heathen, who do not know God; and that in his matter no-one should wrong his brother or take advantage of Him. The Lord will punish men for all such sins, as we have already told you and warned you. (4:3-6)

The basic meaning of the word "holy" is separate; that is separated to God and away from the world. It has little to do with ritual and ceremony. It has more to do with the life we lead and the company we keep. It would seem that some of the Thessalonians had not learnt to control their bodies and the passionate lusts that originate there. This type of behavior was common among the heathen and, of course, some of these Christians had been heathen before their conversion. They had turned form idols to serve the living God and some pagan worship involved temple prostitutes. Homosexuality was a common practice amongst the Greeks, particularly between teacher and pupil. Thus immorality was rife in their culture. The Thessalonian believers needed to be totally separate (holy) from their previous life style.

It would seem that some of the believers were also wronging their Christian brothers. This may refer to advances made to their wives, or propositions put to family members of their family (cf 1 Corinthians 5:1). Such behaviour has no place within the Christian community. When I was first a Christian I was amazed at the number of passages in the epistles which implied that some of the Christians of New Testament times were morally extremely lax. Certainly no Christian today would behave like that! However, the decline in morality over the last thirty years has seen many Christians engulfed in the snares of lust and eroticism, running their lives and that of their families. Such behaviour will be punished by the Lord, writes Paul. But if He is to forgive people all their sins, what punishment will there be?

As well as forgiving believers, granting them eternal life and clothing them with righteousness to serve Him, the Scriptures also speak of rewards, crowns, prizes and the like – a subject I have dealt with more fully in *Gifts and Rewards from God* published by the Open Bible Trust. These are to be awarded to Christians according to their works (e.g. see 1 Corinthians 3:10-15). Thus the punishment will be loss of any such rewards. As Paul states in Ephesians 5:5, "For of this you can be sure: No immoral, impure or greedy person – such a man is an idolater – has no inheritance in the kingdom of Christ and God." This does not mean the man has no eternal life in the kingdom. It means he has no inheritance there. "He himself will be saved, but only as one escaping through the flames"; i.e. with eternal life and no more (1 Corinthians 3:15)

> *For God did not call us to be impure but to live holy lives. Therefore he who rejects this instruction does not reject man but God, who gives you his Holy Spirit. (4:7-8)*

These are strong words from Paul, But God's desire is strong for His servants to live lives which please Him – holy and honourable lives, ones not given to sexual immorality and passionate lust. Permissiveness many be fun in the short term, but in the long run it leaves a wake of unfulfilled and unsatisfactory broken relationships. For society it is even more disastrous, if that is possible. Family life degenerates and slowly disappears. Fewer and fewer children live with both their parents. Child abuse increases as the man about the house is frequently not the natural father. Then there are the sexually transmitted diseases, AIDS being the most disastrous. It must be obvious why God calls us to be pure and to live holy and honourable lives pleasing to Him. Such lives are better for us. Short term passionate pleasures may have to be given up, but the long term benefits in this life alone are worth it, to say nothing of the rewards in the next.

> *Now about brotherly love we do not need to write to you, for you yourselves have been taught by God to love each other. And in fact, you do love all*

the brothers throughout Macedonia. Yet we urge
you, brothers, to do so more and more. (4:9-10)

Some of the Thessalonians may have been lax morally, even to the point of wronging their Christian brothers, but it would seem from these verses, and from elsewhere in the letter, that their behaviour was an example to all. None the less Paul urges them to display more and more love for their brothers.

This is the second time within a few verses that he has urged them "more and more". In 4:1 it was to live lives pleasing to God.

> *Make it your ambition to lead a quiet life, to mind*
> *your own business and work with your hands, just*
> *as we told you, so that your daily life may win*
> *respect of outsiders and so that you will not be*
> *dependent on anybody. (4:11-12)*

It would seem that some in the Thessalonian church were busybodies who did not work and who looked to others for their food. Late, this was to become a greater problem (2 Thessalonians 3:10-12). Possibly because they expected the Lord to return soon, they did not consider it worthwhile to work and go about their own business. Here Paul instructs otherwise. Outsiders would not be won over by watching men idling their time away and begging for food. A more industrious attitude would have a far greater influence upon non-Christians. This is equally true today and there is a similar temptation for believers in the industrialised nations where idleness may be encouraged by the benefits of a welfare state.

> *Brothers, we do not want you to be ignorant about*
> *those who fall asleep, or to grieve like the rest of*

men, who have no hope. We believe that Jesus died
and rose again and so we believe that God will
bring with Jesus those who have fallen asleep in
him. According to the Lord's own word, we tell
you that we who are still alive, who are left till the
coming (parousia) of the Lord, will certainly not
precede those who have fallen asleep. (4:13-15)

Paul uses the term sleep to describe death, as did our Saviour (John 11:11-15; cf. Acts 7:60 and 13:36). However, here and in 1 Corinthians 15:18 he writes of those who are asleep "in Christ" or asleep "in him" to describe believers who have died. Those who trust in Christ are in Christ and they sleep in Christ and He will just as certainly wake them as He woke Lazarus.

It would appear that some of the Thessalonians believers were concerned for the dead. They were expecting Christ's return to be soon, within a matter of years (see earlier). However, some of their number had died. What was going to become of them? Would they miss the return of Christ and not be part of the kingdom He was to establish? Paul explains that they will be part of both. In fact just as Jesus died and rose, so those who had died will rise again. Not only that, believers who are alive at the time of His coming will in no way have preferential treatment over those who have fallen asleep.

Resurrection is assured to all who fall asleep in Christ. They will not be preceded in any way by those who are alive at the time. Notice that Paul did not say that they were not to grieve. He state that he did not want them to "grieve like the rest of men, who have no hope". It is normal and natural to grieve the loss of a loved one. It is right and proper to shed tears at such a time. However, such a loss is a temporary one. The parting is but for a period. As such, Christian grief should not be as great. It should not be like that of people who sadly have no hope. It is with words such as these that the Thessalonians were to comfort any who had suffered the loss of a loved one.

> *For the Lord himself will come down, with a loud command, with the voice of an archangel and with the trumpet call of God, and the dead in Christ will rise first. After that, we who are still alive and are left will be caught up with them in the clouds to meet them Lord in the air. And so we will be with the Lord for ever. Therefore encourage each other with these words. (4:16-20)*

In 1 Corinthians 15 Pau deals with similar matters, which must have been worrying the believers there. He writes to the Corinthian Christians stating that "in Christ all will be made alive". He then goes on to say when this is to take place: "But each in his own turn: Christ, the firstfruits; then, when he comes, those who belong to him" (vs 22-23). He also speaks of those who are dead (asleep) at the time and those who are alive. "Listen, I will tell you a mystery: We will not all sleep, but we will all be changed – in a flash, in the twinkling of an eye, at the last trumpet. For the trumpet will sound, the dead will be raised imperishable, and we will be changed" (vs 51-52).

These passages throw light on each other. Both speak of the coming (*parousia*) of Christ, the trumpet call, the dead in Christ being raised, and believers being changed. "Therefore, my dear brothers, stand firm … Therefore encourage each other with these words" (1 Corinthians 15:58; 1 Thessalonians 4:18).

There are various interpretations of this passage, which are considered in an appendix. Here, however, is not the place to deal with them. Paul's aim in both of these passages is not to give a treatise on the state of the dead or the fate of Christians when Christ returns. Rather it is to encourage and give hope to believers who have suffered the loss of loved ones. At such times wrangling over immortality versus resurrection and pre versus post tribulation eschatology is inappropriate. Words of encouragement are the order of the day.

1 Thessalonians

Chapter 5

Chapter 5

Now, brothers, about times and dates we do not need to write to you, for you know very well that the day of the Lord will come like a thief in the night. While people are saying, "Peace and safety," destruction will come on them suddenly, as labour pains on a pregnant woman, and they will not escape. (5:1-3)

These Thessalonians were privileged to have had Paul teach them about prophetic events. None-the-less, one of the reasons for his second letter was that they have become unsettled and alarmed by some views different from what they had learned from him (2 Thessalonians 2:2).

The day of the Lord is not the return of Christ. It is the subject of the Old Testament prophecy of Joel.

> "What a dreadful day! For the day of the Lord is near; it will come like a destruction from the Almighty ... Blow the trumpet in Zion; sound the alarm on my holy hill. Let all who live in the land tremble, for the day of the Lord is coming ... The day of the Lord is great; it is terrible. Who can endure it? ... I will show wonders in the heavens and on earth, blood and fire and billows of smoke. The sun will be darkened and the moon turned to blood before the coming of the great and dreadful day of the Lord ... For the day of the Lord is near in the valley of decision. The sun and moon will be darkened, and the stars will no longer shine." (Joel 1:15; 2:1,11,31; 3:14).

The day of the Lord warrants a publication to itself and I have dealt with it more fully in *Joel's Prophecy: Past and Future*[1]. However, form what is said above, it is clear that it is a terrible time, especially for those living in Zion and the land of Judea.

Later some of the Thessalonians had difficulty placing the day of the Lord into the prophetic order of events. It would seem that within a short time of this first letter to the Thessalonians Paul had to write a second as these people had become confused over the issue. In 2 Thessalonians 2:2-8 Paul gives a brief scenario of future events, stating that the day of the Lord will not come *until* "the rebellion occurs and the man of lawlessness is revealed". It is these two events which start the day of the Lord. This man is a person who opposes and exalts himself over God and who sets himself up in the Jerusalem temple to be worshipped. He is to be destroyed by Christ at His coming *(parousia)*. From this, and elsewhere, it seems that the day of the Lord describes the period of time leading up to, and possibly including, Christ's return.

From Daniel we can learn more about these times and dates. The subject of Daniel 9:24-27 is a period of seventy sevens, or 490 years. Verse 27 deals with the last seven years at the start of which Israel makes a covenant allowing them to offer their morning and evening sacrifices in the temple. The other party to this covenant is the all-powerful king of the North. This covenant gives Israel the "peace and safety" spoken of in 1 Thessalonians 5:3.

However, in Daniel 11:29-32 we read of a battle between the king of the South and this king of the North. The king of the North is also opposed by ships form the western coastline. At this he loses

---

[1] Published by The Open Bible Trust and aavailable as an eBook from Amazon and Apple and as a KDP paperback from Amazon.

heart, turns, and vents his fury against the covenant he had made with Israel. His armed forces desecrate the temple fortress and he abolishes the daily sacrifices. This may be the rebellion mentioned in 2 Thessalonians 2:3. Next he sets himself up to be worshipped and later has an image of himself placed in the Jerusalem temple (2 Thessalonians 2:4; Revelation 13:14-15).

According to Daniel 9:27 the ending of the sacrifices and offerings is in the middle of the seven years, that is three and a half years after the covenant has been made. (See Daniel 8:11). For the remaining three and a half years this ruler oppresses Israel and attempts to destroy them (Daniel 7:25; 8:23-25; 11:33). At the end of this time his power is taken away and he is destroyed, but not by human hands, rather by the coming Christ (Daniel 7:26-27; 8:25; 9:27; 11:45; 2 Thessalonians 2:8; see also Daniel 2:34-35, 44-45).

Matthew 24 also speaks of the desecration of the temple, warning those in Judea to flee to the mountains, and stating that the period after this destruction will be one of "great distress", unequalled from the beginning of the world until now – and never to be equaled again". This time is brought to an end by the return of Christ (Matthew 24:15-16, 21, 29-30). It would seem that the expression "the day of the Lord" is used to describe the years just prior to the return of Christ.

> *But you, brothers, are not in darkness so that this*
> *day should surprise you like a thief. (5:4)*

Although the day of the Lord will come like a thief in the night for many and will being a destructive end to the "peace and safety" of the people in Jerusalem and Judea, believers who know about the times and the dates should not be taken unawares. That day should not surprise them like a thief. When they see a seven year covenant made with Israel they should be on their guard. When the battle with the king of the South takes place and the ships of the western coastlands join in and the king of the North retreats, then they should hold their breath. The day of the Lord will have begun.

> *You are all sons of the light and sons of the day.*
> *We do not belong to the night or to the darkness.*
> *So then, let us not be like others, who are asleep,*
> *but let us be alert and self-controlled. For those*
> *who sleep, sleep at night, and those who get drunk,*
> *get drunk at night. But since we belong to the day,*
> *let us be self-controlled, putting on faith and love*
> *as a breastplate, and hope of salvation as a*
> *helmet. (5:5-8)*

Paul here uses several figures of speech. The Thessalonian believers are likened to sons of the light and sons of the day. They should not be like those who belong to the darkness and night, who lack self-control, get drunk and who are spiritually asleep. Rather Christians should be spiritually awake, self-controlled, putting on faith, love and hope. They should live as the sons of the light. They should not give in to temptation. They have their faith, their love and their hope of salvation. These will protect them like a helmet and a breastplate, and will see them through the great and terrible day of the Lord which ends when Christ returns and their hope is realised.

> *For God did not appoint us to suffer wrath but to*
> *receive salvation through our Lord Jesus Christ.*
> *He died for us so that whether we are awake or*
> *asleep, we may live together with him. Therefore*

encourage one another and build each other up,
just in fact as you are doing. (5:9-11)

The Thessalonians need not fear the wrath of God. It is to fall
only upon those who oppose Him. His plan for believers was, and
is, salvation through Jesus Christ. Whether awake or asleep,
spiritually, they will live together with Him. Therefore, writes
Paul for the second time, "encourage one another". His purpose
this time was for the Thessalonians to build each other up; for
those who are spiritually awake to help encourage those who had
been pulled towards the darkness and night.

> *Now we ask you, brothers, to respect those who*
> *work hard among you, who are over you in the*
> *Lord and who admonish you. Hold them in*
> *highest regard in love because of their work. Live*
> *in peace with each other. (5:12-13)*

It would appear that the authority of the leaders of the church at
Thessalonica was being undermined by some of the believers
there. At that time such leaders were appointed by the Holy Spirit
(Acts 20:28). Paul instructs the Thessalonians to respect those
who were over them in the Lord and to hold them in high regard.
In this age people appoint other people to positions of authority (1
Timothy 3:1-12); Titus 1:5-9). None-the-less, they, too, need to
be respected and held in the highest regard "because of their
work". Neither the leaders of the Thessalonian Church nor
Christian leaders today are without their shortcomings. However,
far more is achieved by care and concern than by criticism and
condemnation.

> *And we urge you, brothers, warn those who are*
> *idle and encourage the weak, be patient with*

everyone. Make sure that nobody pays back
wrong for wrong, but always try to be kind to
each other and to everyone else. (5:14-15)

The most obvious yet important point here is that these words are
addressed to all the Thessalonian believers, not solely to the
leadership. It is the Christian duty of all to urge, warn, encourage,
help, be patient. So often these are left to just the ministers or
pastors.

Paul instructs all not to retaliate, urging them not only to be kind
to one another, but to be kind to everyone.

Be joyful always; pray continually; give thanks
in all circumstances, for this is God's will for
you in Christ Jesus. (5:16-18)

In chapter 4:13 Paul wrote that he did not want those who
had lost a loved one "to grieve, like the rest of men, who have no
hope". It would be natural to grieve, but there was no need for
despair. However, when such losses occur it is not only natural,
right and proper to be sad and sorrowful. That being the case, how
can we be expected to "be joyful always"? In 5:16-18 Paul uses
"always", "continually", and "in all circumstances", and if we
take these words at their face value then the Thessalonians were
exhorted to practice the impossible.

It would seem that Paul is encouraging them to be joyful,
prayerful and thankful in the normal course of events. This should
be the natural disposition of a believer in Christ. There will be
times of sadness. There will be occasions to mourn. However, in
the usual circumstances of day to day living we should be joyful,
prayerful and thankful.

Do not put out the Spirit's fire; do not treat prophecies with contempt. Test everything. Hold on to the good. Avoid every kind of evil. (5:19-22)

Although the work of the Holy Spirit may vary form one dispensation to another, it would appear that He does not force Himself upon people. King Saul's behaviour was so bad that the Holy Spirit departed (1 Samuel 16:14), and David feared the same was to happen to him (Psalm 51:11). During the Acts dispensation the spirits of the prophets were subject to the control of the prophets (1 Corinthians 14:32) and here, in 1 Thessalonians 5:19 it would seem that they were in danger of quenching the Spirit. Just as it is possible to silence our God-given consciences (1 Timothy 4:2) so, too, can believers in all ages silence the God-given Spirit. Sadly Timothy, such a tower of strength to the Thessalonians, in later life needed exhortations from Paul to use his Spirit-given gifts (1 Timothy 1:18; 4:14; 2 Timothy 1:16). And it is possible for us today to grieve the Spirit rather than to be filled by Him (Ephesians 4:30; 5:8).

At the time Thessalonians was written various believers had the gift of prophecy. This did not necessarily entail speaking of the future. A prophet was one who told forth, rather than fore told. Much of what the prophets said was to do with what God had done and was doing, rather than what He was going to do. As such, and with man's insatiable curiosity about the future, it would seem that the Thessalonians were treating such prophecies with contempt. In this they were not unlike the Corinthians whom Paul urged to "Follow the way of love and eagerly desire spiritual gifts, especially the gift of prophecy" (1 Corinthians 14:1; nb vs 1-5).

Next Paul instructs them to test everything and for us who have a completed Bible we should test all things against the Scriptures. However, the Thessalonians were in a different position and here Paul may be referring to the Acts period gifts of testing those who prophesied and of discerning between good and evil spirits (1 John 4:1-3; 1 Corinthians 12"10). The result of the test should tell them whether or not the prophecy was from God, and if it was the should hold on to the good. If it was not, they should avoid it.

> *May God himself, the God of peace, sanctify you through and through. May your whole spirit, soul and body be kept blameless at the coming of our Lord Jesus Christ. The one who calls you is faithful and he will do it. (5:23-24)*

Avoiding every kind of evil (v22) is what God would have all believers do, for His desire is for our whole spirit, soul and body to be kept blameless. However, it is impossible for believers to achieve this and it is God Himself Who sanctifies us through and through. He has promised to do this for all who have placed their faith in Christ for forgiveness. He has promised it and He will do it for He is faithful. Such will be the happy state of all the redeemed on resurrection.

> *Brother, pray for us. Greet all the brothers with a holy kiss. I charge you before the Lord to have this letter read to all the brothers. The grace of our Lord Jesus Christ be with you. (5:25-28)*

As he nears the end of his letter Paul urges them to greet one another in the customary manner of their society, namely a kiss. Nobody was to pay back wrong with wrong. They were to be kind to one another. They were to greet one another. Also they were to be sure that all heard the contents of this letter.

Two things are common to the ending of many of Paul's epistles. First is the request from prayer for himself. Even though this man was chosen by God to be His apostle, teacher, and minister to the Gentiles, yet Paul felt the need of prayer. In this letter the request is unqualified. In others, like Colossians, it was that God may open a door for the message of the mystery of Christ and that Paul may proclaim it clearly as he should (Colossians 4:3-4). How appropriate a prayer for today.

The second is a reference to grace. Here it is that "the grace of our Lord Jesus Christ be with you". What an appropriate salutation for us today. Where would any of us be without the grace of God and His forgiveness, redemption, salvation, eternal life and righteousness? All these, and so much more, are free and undeserved gracious gifts acquired and secured for us by our Lord and Saviour, Jesus Christ. He Who know no sin became a sin offering for us so that in Him we might become righteousness of God (2 Corinthians 5:21). To Him be all glory, honour and praise.

Appendix 1:

1 Thessalonians 4:14-18

Appendix 1:
1 Thessalonians 4:14-18

We believe that Jesus died and rose again and so we believe that God will bring with Jesus those who have fallen asleep in him. According to the Lord's own word, we tell you we who are still alive, who are left till the coming (parousia) of the Lord, will certainly not precede those which have fallen asleep. For the Lord himself will come down from heaven, with a loud command, with the voice of the archangel and with the trumpet call of God, and the dead in Christ will rise first. After that, we who are still alive and are left will be caught up with them in the clouds to meet the Lord in the air. And so we will be with the Lord for ever.

One view of this passage which is held in many Christian circles is that here Paul is not talking about Christ's second coming to the earth, but rather His coming in the air to rapture the church and take it back to heaven. We shall discuss this interpretation.

Parousia

One of the key words in this passage is *parousia*, defined as follows by Walter Bauer, *A Greek-English Lexicon of the New Testament*, as follows:

1. presence…
2. coming, advent as in the first stage of presence…
    a.   of human beings, in the usual sense…

b. in a special technical sense... of Christ. *Parousia* became the official term for a visit of a person of high rank, especially of kings and emperors visiting a province... nearly always of his Messianic Advent in glory to judge the world at the end of this age

W E Vine, in his *Expository Dictionary of New Testament Words,* defines *parousia* as follows:

> literally, a presence, *para*, with, and *ousia*, being (from *eimi*, to be), denotes both the arrival and a consequent presence with. For instance, in a papyrus letter a lady speaks of the necessity of her *parousia* in a place in order to attend to matters relating to her property there. Paul speaks of his *parousia* in Philippi, Phil. 2:12 (in contrast to his *apousia*, his absence).

Hence *parousia* refers to an "advent" and a consequent "presence with". It clearly relates to Christ's second coming, His return to the earth, in a number of places. For example see Matthew 24:3, 27, 37, 39 where the disciples wanted to know what would be the sign of His coming (*parousia*) and of the end of the age. There Christ explains to them a number of events, including the great tribulation (KJV), distress (NIV), which is to precede His coming (*parousia*): (note verses 15-31 and cp. Vs 21 and 30). Similarly in 2 Thessalonians 2:3-8 Paul describes what must happen before the (*parousia*) of Christ. Both of these unambiguous passages show clearly that the *parousia* follows the tribulation.

If that be the case how is it that some say that the coming (*parousia*) of 1 Thessalonians 4:15 precedes the tribulation? To justify this Vine defines three aspects of the coming (*parousia*) or Christ.

> When used of the return of Christ, at the Rapture of the Church, it signifies, not merely His momentary coming for His saints, but His presence with them from that moment until His revelation and manifestation to the world.
>
> In some passages the word give prominence to the beginning of that period, the course of the period being implied, 1 Cor. 15:23; 1 Thess. 4:15; 5:23; 2 Thess. 2:1; Jas. 5:7,8; 2 Pet. 3:4.
>
> In some, the course is prominent, Matt. 24:3, 37; 1 Thess. 3:13; 1 John 2:28;
>
> In others the conclusion of the period, Matt. 24:27; 2 Thess. 2:8.

This is far from clear! According to Vine in 2 Thessalonians 2 *parousia* refers to the beginning of some period in verse 1, and to its conclusion in verse 8! Similarly in Matthew 24 where it takes on a different meaning in verses 3 and 37 to that in verse 27!

Also, *Parousia* refers to "a person of high rank … visiting a province" and to his "arrival and consequent presence" there. Thus the view that the "coming" of 1 Thessalonians 4:15 is "momentary" and predates the tribulation cannot be correct for it has Christ's arrival and presence, and hence His visit to His kingdom, some years *after* His coming!

The archangel, trumpets and clouds

It has been said that such passages as Matthew 24 relate to the Lord's return to the mount of Olives, to the earth and to Israel, whereas 1 Thessalonians 4:14-17 relates to His coming in air for the "Gentile Church" of this dispensation. Thus the former is very Jewish and the latter non-Jewish. However, if we investigate this what do we find?

First there is the voice of the archangel in 1 Thessalonians 4:16. Scripture knows of only one archangel, namely Michael (Jude 9), who is intimately connected with Israel, being called its prince (Daniel 10:31, 21; 12:1).

Next we read of the trumpet call, also verse 16. Trumpets are again associated with Israel and with its Feast of Trumpets (Leviticus 23:23-25). Also 1 Corinthians 15:52 indicates that this raising of the dead takes place at the sounding of the *last* trumpet, which Revelation 11:15 links with the time when "The kingdom of the world has become the kingdom of our Lord and of his Christ". A state of affairs that occurs when He returns to this earth to set up His kingdom.

Then there is the mention of clouds which the Lord Himself connects with His return to the earth in Matthew 24:30 and which the Jews associated with the coming of the Messiah (Matthew 26:64-66). Clouds are also linked with His coming back to the earth in Acts 1:9-11 when He was taken up into a cloud at His ascension and the disciples were told He would return in like manner. And Revelation 1:7 states, "Look, he is coming with the clouds".

To meet

Lastly, there is the word "meet", literally "meeting". Of this Greek word, *apantesis, Moulton says:*

> It is used in the papyri of a newly arriving magistrate. "It seems that the special idea of the word was the official welcome of a newly arrived dignitary" (Moulton, *Greek Testament Grammar* Vol. 1, p. 14).

This is a word most appropriate for our Lord, who will be a new arriving dignitary after years of absence. It comes from the word *apantao* which, according to Bullinger's *Greek Lexicon and Concordance* means:

> ... to come or go from a place towards a person; and so meet face to face from opposite directions; especially to meet and come back with the person met.

This is how the word is used in both Matthew 25:6 and Acts 28:15. In the former the reason why the virgins went out with their lamps to *meet* the bridegroom was to light his path *back* to the house. Similarly in the latter, where the brothers from Rome went out to the Three Taverns to *meet* Paul and *return* with him to Rome.

It would seem that 1 Thessalonians 4:14-17 teaches that the dead are raised, the living are changed, both are taken up into the air to meet the Lord and both *come back* with Him to the earth. All this is to happen at His coming (*parousia*).

Historical setting

However, perhaps the most powerful argument in favour of 1 Thessalonians 4:14-18 relating to Christ's return to earth is to place the passage in its context.

Matthew 24 is a passage I have dealt with at length in *Signs of the Second Coming*[2]. There Christ describes events which culminate with His return to the earth (v 30). He also adds that all this could have happened within the lifetime of that generation (v 34).

Peter opens Acts by telling the Jews that if they repented and turned to God their sins would be wiped out, the times of refreshing would come, and Christ would return (Acts 3:19-21). The imminent return of Christ to the earth was a possibility throughout the period covered by the Acts of the Apostles and many of the letters written during that time reflect this. For example, James considers the "The Lord's coming is near" (5:8). 1 Peter 4:7 states that "The end of all things is near" and 1 John 2:18 that "This is the last hour". Hebrews 10:37 has "For in just a very little while, he who is coming will come and will not delay".

In writing to the Corinthians Paul states that "The time is short" and that "The fulfilment of the ages has come" (7:29; 10:11). In Romans 13:12 he wrote that "The night is nearly over; the day is almost here".

Now both 1 and 2 Thessalonians were written before Corinthians Romans and Hebrews, and before the letters of Peter and John. They were probably written soon after James penned his epistle. That being the case we need to read Thessalonians in the light of

---

[2] Published by The Open Bible Trust and available as an eBook from Amazon and Apple and a KDP paperback from Amazon.

this historical context, namely that what was expected at that time was the imminent return of Christ to the earth, His coming (*parousia*) on clouds to end the great tribulation. This is the subject of 2 Thessalonians 2:3-8 and the logical and most obvious conclusion is that it is also the subject of 1 Thessalonians 4:14-18. Whether or not Christians in this dispensation are to be raptured before Christ's return is not the subject of this treatise. What I wish to establish here is but two points.

1. 1 Thessalonians 4:14-18 refers to Christ's return to the earth. This is clear for *parousia* is linked with the voice of the archangel Michael (Israel's prince), the trumpet call and clouds. Also the dead who are raised, and the living, who are changed, go out to meet the Lord in the air and return with Him to the earth.

2. If we are consistent *parousia* always refers to Christ's return to this earth, His arrival here and His permanent dwelling with His people here from then onwards.

Appendix 2:

The dead in Christ will rise

Appendix 2:
The dead in Christ will rise

1 Thessalonians 4:14-18 contain two verses which may summarise the two differing views held in evangelical Christendom with respect to the state of the dead.

> *We believe that Jesus died and rose again and so we believe that God will bring with Jesus those who have fallen asleep in him. (4:14)*

> *For the Lord himself will come down from heaven, with a loud command, with the voice of the archangel and with the trumpet call of God, and the dead in Christ will rise first. (4:16)*

The section of Christendom which holds that part of man is immortal and that on death a believer goes to be with the Lord quotes verse 14 to support that view, stating that on His return "God will bring with Jesus those who have fallen asleep in him". Their interpretation of this verse is that those who have fallen asleep in Jesus have been in heaven with Him since death, and so Christ can bring them with Him.

However, the section of Christendom which holds that no part of man is inherently immortal quotes verse 16 to support its view, stating that those who are dead are asleep in Jesus and do not wake until God raises them at Christ's return. At that time they are taken up into the air to meet the Lord Who brings them with Him back to the earth.

More light on this may be obtained from a closer look at 1 Corinthians 15. There we read that the dead are to be raised at Christ's second coming (v 23 and cf. Revelation 20:4-6). Then, later in the chapter, Paul writes:

> *Listen, I tell you a mystery: We will not fall asleep, but we will be changed – in a flash, in the twinkling of an eye, at the last trumpet. For the trumpet will sound,* the dead will be raised imperishable, and we will be changed. For the perishable must clothe itself with the imperishable, and *the mortal with immortality. When the perishable has been clothed with the imperishable, and* the mortal with immortality, *then the saying that is written will come true: "Death has been swallowed up in victory."* (1 Corinthians 15:51-54)

It would seem here that immortality is not put on by man until resurrection. If he has immortality *now*, then it can be said *now* that "Death has been swallowed up in victory," a state of affairs that is painfully not the case. Man may seek immortality (Romans 2:7), but God is the only One Who has it (1 Timothy 6:16) and, wonder of wonders, through His grace and love He shares this immortality with believers when He raises them from the dead.

This being the case, it would seem that in 1 Thessalonians 4:14-18 Paul says something similar to what he does in 1 Corinthians 15. There it is clear that the mortal puts on immortality when raised from than at Christ's return. Similarly, it is at resurrection, rather than at death, that a person becomes imperishable. Here, too, those who are asleep in Jesus are awakened when the Lord raises them from the dead. They rise to meet Christ in the air and

He brings them back with Him to the earth. This appears to be the
most consistent interpretation of this passage.

About the author

Michael Penny was born in Ebbw Vale, Gwent, Wales in 1943. He read Mathematics at the University of Reading, before teaching for twelve years and becoming the Director of Mathematics and Business Studies at Queen Mary's College Basingstoke in Hampshire, England. In 1978 he entered Christian publishing, and in 1984 became the administrator of the Open Bible Trust.

He held this position for seven years, before moving to the USA and becoming pastor of Grace Church in New Berlin, Wisconsin. He returned to Britain in 1999, and is at present the Administrator and Editor of The Open Bible Trust. In 2010 he was elected Chairman of Churches Together in Reading, where he speaks in a number of churches. He is the lead chaplain at Reading College and is on the Advisory Committee of Reading University Christian Union.

He lives near Reading with his wife and has appeared on BBC Radio Berkshire and Premier Radio a number of times. He has made several speaking tours of America, Canada, Australia, New Zealand and the Netherlands, as well as ones to South Africa and the Philippines. Some of his writings have been translated into German and Russian.

As well as writing articles for *Search* magazine and many Bible study booklets, he has also written several major books including: *The Manual on the Gospel of John; 40 Problem Passages;*

Approaching the Bible; Galatians - Interpretation and Application; The Miracles of the Apostles; Introducing God's Word (with Carol Brown and Lynn Mrotek); *Introducing God's Plan* (with Sylvia Penny).

Recent books are *The Bible! Myth or Message?, Joel's Prophecy: Past and Future* and *The Balanced Christian Life* (based on Ephesians, and is designed for use with Lent Studies and House Group Bible Studies).

His latest three books are:

- James: His life and letter
- Peter: His life and letters
- Paul: A Missionary of Genius

Details of these books, and other writings, can be seen at

www.obt.org.uk

There are over 40 books written by Michael Penny.

These can be seen at

wwww.obt.org.uk/michael-penny

Michael Penny is editor of *Search* magazine

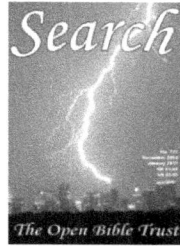

Also in this Series

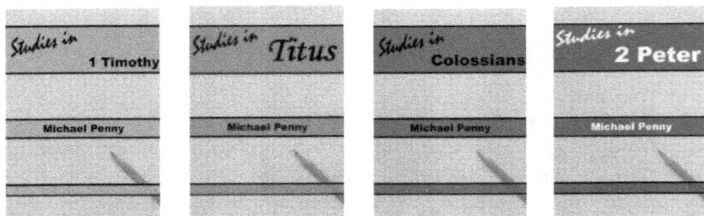

Michael Penny has written a number of other books in this series including:

- **Studies in 1 Thessalonians**
- **Studies in 2 Thessalonians**
- **Studies in Colossians**
- **Studies in Philemon**
- **Studies in 1 Timothy**
- **Studies in 2 Timothy**
- **Studies in Titus**
- **Studies in 2 Peter**
- **Studies in John's Epistles**
- **Studies in Jude**
- **Studies in Ruth**

Further details can be seen on

www.obt.org.uk

Further details of all publications mentioned on these pages
can be seen on the website

www.obt.org.uk

They can be ordered from that website.

They are also available
as eBooks from Amazon and Apple

and as KDP paperbacks from Amazon.

Also by Michael Penny

Following Philippians

W M Henry and Michael Penny

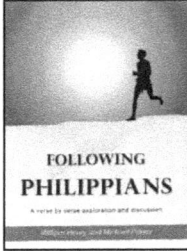

This is much more than a commentary on Philippians. The authors first examine what the passage would have meant to the original readers in Philippi, before seeking an application for Christians today. They do this by dividing each chapter of this into a number of sections.

FOLLOWING PHILIPPIANS

- First the *Big Issues* set out the main points of the passage of Philippians being considered.
- Then the passage is *Explored* with helpful insights into the historical setting of first century Philippi and the issues of that day.
- This is followed by a set of *Comprehension questions,* for personal meditation or group discussion.
- Next the passages is *Discussed* in a manner which takes what has been learnt and directs light on the experiences of Christians in the 21st Century.
- Each chapter of the book concludes with a set of *Contemplation Questions*, again for personal meditation or group discussion.

The result is a study guide to Philippians which balances well researched historical information with practical lessons for today's Christians.

About this book

Studies in
1 Thessalonians

1 Thessalonians is one of Paul's earliest letters, written to the saint sin Thessalonica just a month or so after he had been forced to leave them after just a few weeks with them. His care and concern for them is very evident in this letter.

Like many of Paul's letters, 1 Thessalonians is a beautiful blend of doctrine and practice, with many exhortations and much encouragement.

This publication begins by giving the historical setting, in a helpful and informative manner, which does much to bring the letter alive for the Christian of today.